KINDERGARTEN

R

AGES 5–6

Math Concepts
Learning Fun Workbook

For information about permission to reproduce selections from this book for
an entire school or school district, please contact permissions@highlights.com.

Published by Highlights Learning • 815 Church Street • Honesdale, Pennsylvania 18431
ISBN: 978-1-68437-283-6
Mfg. 05/2020
Printed in Brainerd, MN, USA
First edition
10 9 8 7 6 5 4

For assistance in the preparation of this book, the editors would like to thank:
Vanessa Maldonado, MSEd; MS Literacy Ed. K–12; Reading/LA Consultant Cert.; K–5 Literacy Instructional Coach
Kristin Ward, MS Curriculum, Instruction, and Assessment; K–5 Mathematics Instructional Coach
Jump Start Press, Inc.

0

zero

This is the number 0.

This is the word **zero**.

This is one way to show 0.

Trace the number **0**. Then write your own.

Trace the word **zero**. Then write your own.

zero

Circle the spaceship with **0** aliens inside. Then draw a line between the 2 spaceships that match.

1
one

This is the number 1.

This is the word one.

This is one way to show 1.

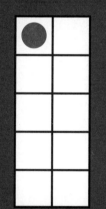

Trace the number 1. Then write your own.

Trace the word **one**. Then write your own.

one

Find and count 1 purple bird and 1 carrot. What other groups of 1 do you see?

Help Bella find her way home. Follow the path to her dad.

2

two

This is the number 2.

This is the word **two**.

This is one way to show 2.

Trace the number **2**. Then write your own.

2 2

Trace the word **two**. Then write your own.

two

Find and count **2** eggs in the top picture. What other groups of **2** do you see?

Circle the differences you see between these pictures.

3
three

This is the number 3.

This is the word three.

This is one way to show 3.

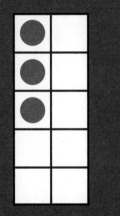

Name 3 things you like to do in the summer.

Trace the number **3**. Then write your own.

3 3

Trace the word **three**. Then write your own.

three

Find and count **3** ladybugs and **3** bees. What other groups of **3** do you see?

4
four

This is the number 4.

This is the word **four**.

This is one way to show 4.

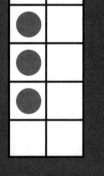

Trace the number 4. Then write your own.

Trace the word **four**. Then write your own.

four

Find and count 4 cherries. What other groups of 4 do you see?

Find and circle the 4 objects in this Hidden Pictures® puzzle.

 airplane

 bucket

 hat

nail

5

five

This is the number 5.

This is the word five.

This is one way to show 5.

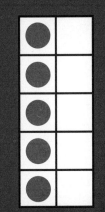

Trace the number **5**. Then write your own.

5   5

Trace the word **five**. Then write your own.

five

Count the number of bears in the family. What other groups of **5** do you see?

Draw a line from each bear to his or her chair.

More or Less

In each row, circle the group that has more dinosaurs.

Compare Numbers: More

Make Five

Count the cupcakes in each box. Draw a line between the pairs of boxes that together contain **5** cupcakes.

Each cupcake has one that matches it exactly. Find each matching pair.

6
six

This is the number 6.

This is the word six.

This is one way to show 6.

What other groups of 6 do you see?

Trace the number **6**. Then write your own.

Trace the word **six**. Then write your own.

six

Find and count **6** pigeons in this scene.

Shoes Required

7

seven

This is the number 7.

This is the word **seven**.

This is one way to show 7.

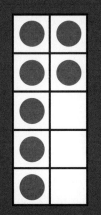

Find and circle 7 7's in this picture.

Trace the number **7**. Then write your own.

7 7

Trace the word **seven**. Then write your own.

seven

Count the **7** tigers in the picture.

8

eight

This is the number 8.

This is the word **eight**.

This is one way to show 8.

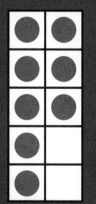

How many arms does an octopus have?

Trace the number **8**. Then write your own.

8 8

Trace the word **eight**. Then write your own.

eight

Count the **8** octopuses. Then draw a line from each octopus to the one that matches it exactly.

9
nine

This is the number 9.

This is the word **nine**.

This is one way to show 9.

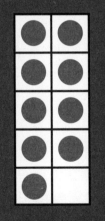

Trace the number **9**. Then write your own.

9   9

Trace the word **nine**. Then write your own.

nine

How many llamas are at the sleepover?

Can you find at least 9 differences between these pictures?

10

ten

This is the number 10.

This is the word ten.

This is one way to show 10.

Trace the number 10. Then write your own.

10 10

Trace the word **ten**. Then write your own.

ten

Find and count 10 lizards.

Make Ten

Count the fish in the tank. Draw more fish to make **10**.

Color the fish. Draw some plants and other things you might see in a fish tank.

11

eleven

This is the number 11.

This is the word **eleven**.

This is one way to show 11.

Trace the number 11. Then write your own.

Trace the word **eleven**.

eleven

Count the doughnuts on the plate. Cross them off as you go. Then draw a line between each pair of doughnuts that look exactly the same.

Circle the doughnut that does not have a match.

12

twelve

This is the number 12.

This is the word twelve.

This is one way to show 12.

Trace the number **12**. Then write your own.

12 12

Trace the word **twelve**.

twelve

Count and circle **12** ice-cream treats in this scene.

Can you find the hidden carrot?

13
thirteen

This is the number 13.

This is the word thirteen.

This is one way to show 13.

Trace the number 13. Then write your own.

13 13

Trace the word **thirteen**.

thirteen

Count and circle 13 birds.

What else can you count in this picture?

14

fourteen

This is the number 14.

This is the word fourteen.

This is one way to show 14.

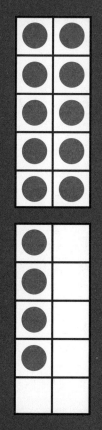

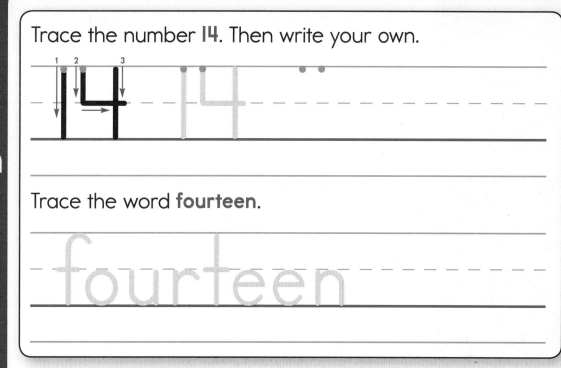

Trace the number 14. Then write your own.

Trace the word **fourteen**.

fourteen

Find and circle all 14 carrots hiding in this picture.

15

fifteen

This is the number 15.

This is the word fifteen.

This is one way to show 15.

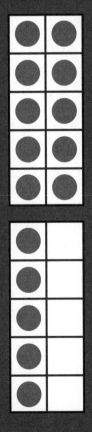

Trace the number 15. Then write your own.

15

Trace the word **fifteen**.

fifteen

Count the **15** jars of candy. Cross them off as you go. Then find and count 15 lollipops.

16
sixteen

This is the number 16.

This is the word sixteen.

This is one way to show 16.

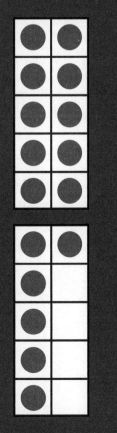

Trace the number **16**. Then write your own.

Trace the word **sixteen**.

Count **16** snowflakes in these two pictures. Place an **X** over each one you find.

Can you find 16 differences between these pictures?

17
seventeen

This is the number 17.

This is the word seventeen.

This is one way to show 17.

Trace the number 17. Then write your own.

17 17

Trace the word seventeen.

seventeen

Count 17 letter blocks. Remember to cross off as you go.

Find and circle the 4 objects in this Hidden Pictures® puzzle.

french fry   bell   horseshoe   pencil

18
eighteen

This is the number 18.

This is the word **eighteen**.

This is one way to show 18.

Trace the number **18**. Then write your own.

18 18

Trace the word **eighteen**.

eighteen

Count and circle 18 pigs. Are there more pigs in the water or on the sand?

Find and circle the **7** objects in this Hidden Pictures® puzzle.

sailboat   carrot   spoon   iron   teacup   toothbrush   candle

19
nineteen

This is the number 19.

This is the word nineteen.

This is one way to show 19.

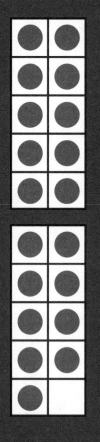

Trace the number **19**. Then write your own.

19 19

Trace the word **nineteen**.

nineteen

Count 19 flowers. Cross out as you go.

Find and circle the **4** objects in this Hidden Pictures® puzzle.

glove   belt   apple core   doughnut

20

twenty

This is the number 20.

This is the word **twenty**.

This is one way to show 20.

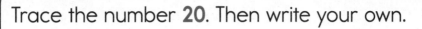

Trace the number **20**. Then write your own.

20 20

Trace the word **twenty**.

twenty

Count and circle **20** balloons.

Are there more red balloons or blue balloons?

Dive In!

How many of Freddy's friends are at the pond today? Find out by writing the missing numbers in the boxes.

1 ☐ ☐ 4 ☐
☐ 6 9 10 13
☐ 19 14 17 16
21 ☐ 23

If you need help, look at the number chart on the inside back cover of this book.

Fair Way

Help Kate and Grandpa find their way to the fair! Write the missing numbers in the boxes.

Squirrel Away

Help Squeaky gather acorns by writing the missing numbers in the boxes.

51

53

56

61

57

63

66

73

70

75

If you need help, look at the number chart on the inside back cover of this book.

Counting Sheep

Fill in the missing numbers from 76 to 100.

Count by 10's

Count by 10's to fill in the missing numbers.

10, 20, ___, ___

50, ___, ___

80, ___, 100

Track 10

How many cereal boxes are here? Color in a square for every box that you see.

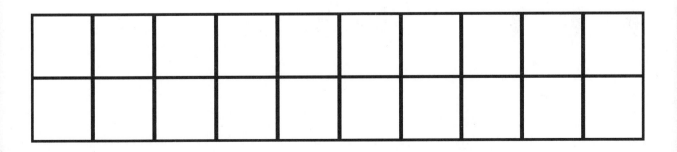

Animal Addition

Count the animals in the first group and write the number. Count the animals in the second group and write the number. How many animals are in both groups all together? We did one to get you started.

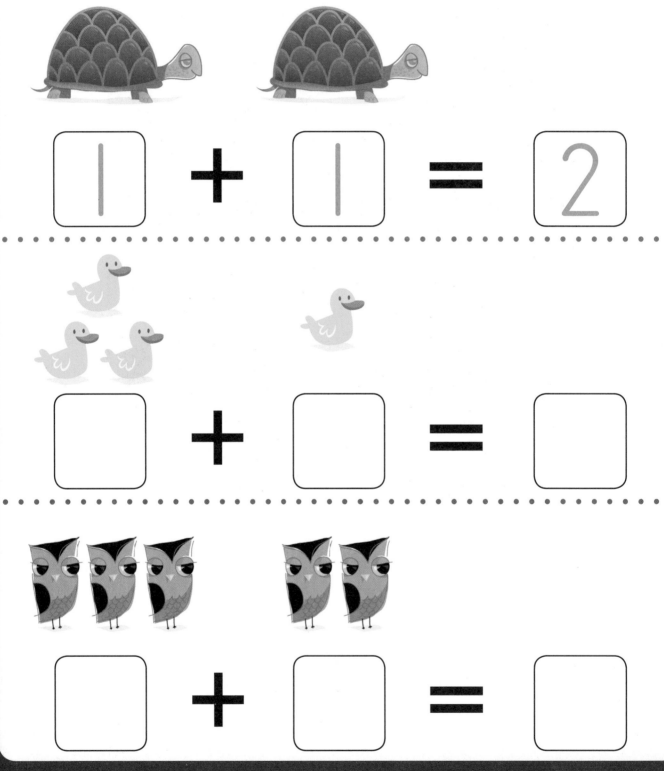

Domino Addition

Count the dots on the first domino and write the number. Count the dots on the second domino and write the number. How many dots are on both dominos in all? We did one to get you started.

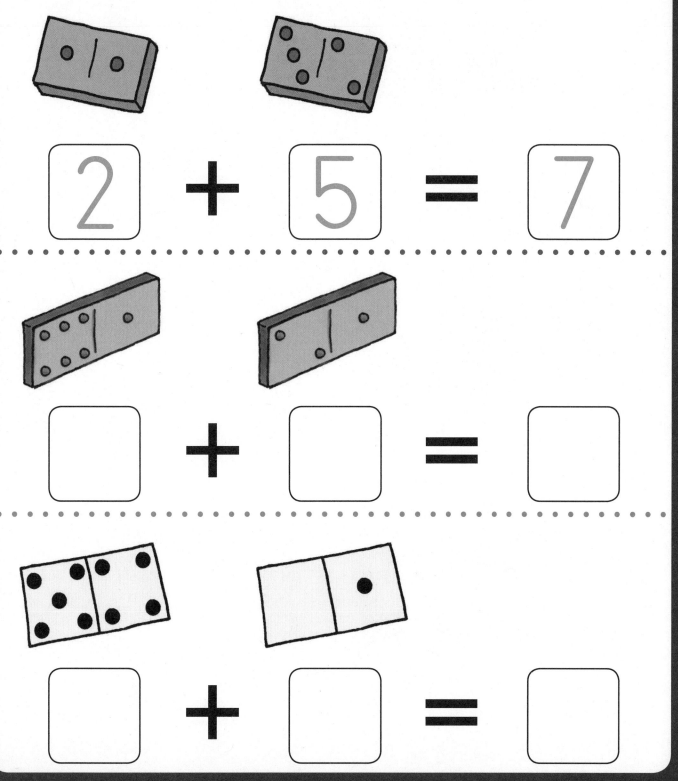

Truck Subtraction

Count the trucks in each group. Write the number. Then cross out **1** truck. How many are left? We did one to get you started.

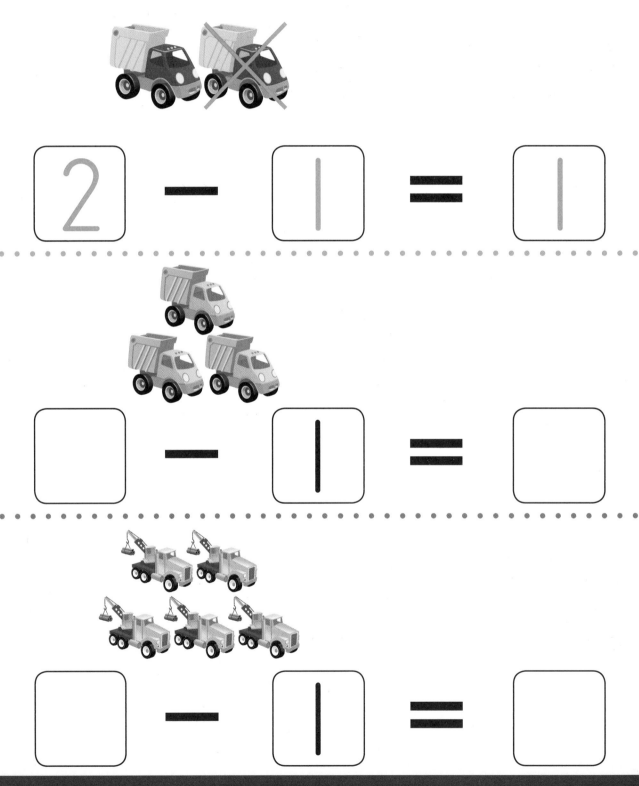

2 − 1 = 1

☐ − 1 = ☐

☐ − 1 = ☐

Candle Subtraction

Count the candles on each cake. Write the number. Then cross out the number of candles indicated. How many are left? We did one to get you started.

$6 - 2 = 4$

☐ $- 2 =$ ☐

☐ $- 4 =$ ☐

Circle

A circle is round. Trace the circle. Then draw your own.

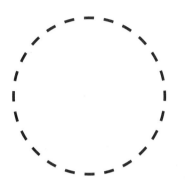

Draw a circle around each circle you see.

How many silly things do you see?

Square

A square has 4 sides that are the same. Trace the square.
Then draw your own.

Draw a square around each square you see. What shape is below the flower? What other shapes do you see?

How many bananas do you see in the picture?

Rectangle

A rectangle has 2 long sides that are the same and 2 short sides that are the same. Trace the rectangle. Then draw your own.

Draw a rectangle around each rectangle you see. What other four-sided shape is above the rabbit cage?

How many of each object do you see in the picture? We did one to get you started.

ruler	1
plant	2
book	3
clock	4
pencil	5
rabbit	6

Triangle

A triangle has 3 sides. Trace the triangle. Then draw your own.

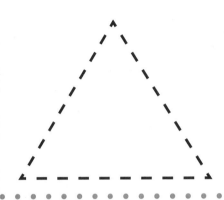

Draw a triangle around each triangle you see.

How many balloons do you see? How many party hats?

Rhombus

A rhombus is like a stretched square. Trace the rhombus. Then draw your own.

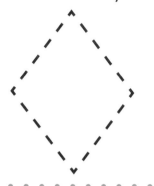

Draw a rhombus around each rhombus you see.

Oval

An oval is like a stretched circle. Trace the oval. Then draw your own.

Draw an oval around each oval you see. What other shapes do you see?

Find and circle the 8 objects in this Hidden Pictures® puzzle.

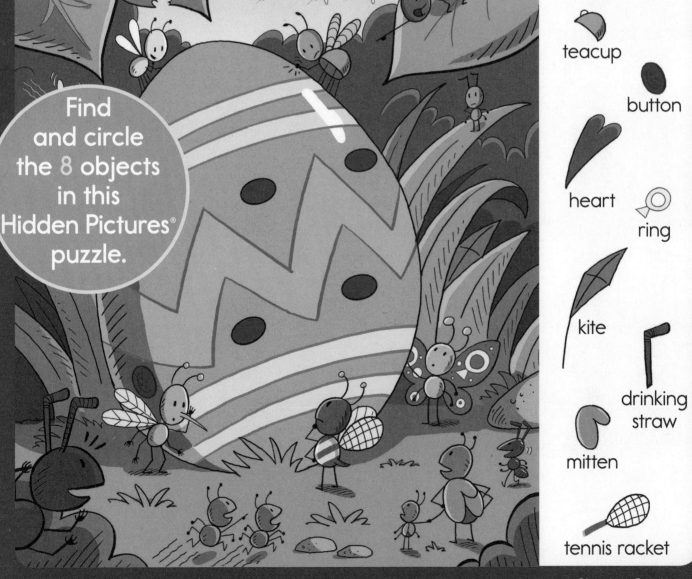

teacup

button

heart

ring

kite

drinking straw

mitten

tennis racket

Short and Tall

Look at all the animals in this picture. Circle the giraffe that is the tallest. Circle the elephant that is the shortest.

Find 5 mittens hidden in this picture.

Color in a mitten for each one you find in the big picture.

Compare by Size

Large and Small

Circle the smallest tree.

Circle the largest bird.

On the Street

Remember to cross off as you count.

How many cars and trucks do you see in this scene?

EXIT

Circle the dog walker with the most dogs.

How many bikes do you see?

How many dogs do you see?

K KINDERGARTEN

Highlights™

Congratulations!

_____
(your name)

worked hard
and finished the

Math Concepts

Learning Fun Workbook

FiNish

Answers

Page 2
Zero

Page 4
Two

Page 6
Four

Page 9
Make 5

Page 11
Seven

Page 13
Nine

Page 14
Ten

Page 19
Fourteen

Page 21
Sixteen

Answers

Page 22
Seventeen

Page 23
Eighteen

Page 24
Nineteen

Page 25
Twenty

There are more red balloons (8) than blue balloons (7).

Page 38
Rectangle

ruler — 1
plant — 2
book — 3
clock — 4
pencil — 5
rabbit — 6

Page 32
Animal Addition

$1 + 1 = 2$
$3 + 1 = 4$
$3 + 2 = 5$

Page 33
Domino Addition

$2 + 5 = 7$
$7 + 3 = 10$
$9 + 1 = 10$

Page 34
Truck Subtraction

$2 - 1 = 1$
$3 - 1 = 2$
$5 - 1 = 4$

Page 35
Candle Subtraction

$6 - 2 = 4$
$7 - 2 = 5$
$9 - 4 = 5$

Page 41
Oval

Page 42
Short and Tall

Pages 44–45
On the Street

There are 12 cars and trucks.

There are 5 bikes.

There are 9 dogs.

The dog walker crossing the street has the most dogs.